ETCHED OR INKED

AN ANTHOLOGY OF POETRY

ARSHIA GAUR

/ BookLeaf
Publishing

India | USA | UK

Made with ❤ on the BookLeaf Publishing Platform
www.bookleafpub.in
www.bookleafpub.com

Dedication

To everyone who ever loved and lost,
and to the one whose silence became my verses.
To scars that learned to speak,
To you, dear reader:
You're heard for the next few pages.

Preface

Poetry is often mistaken for finished art: something to be consumed all at once, neat and complete. But these poems never lived that way. They were scribbled on scraps of paper, typed into phones during restless nights, in empty rooms where no one else was listening.

Somehow, those scattered fragments began to push back. They didn't just hold my thoughts; they held me. They became a conversation between who I was, who I longed to become, and the chaotic world that kept spinning while I tried to catch it in words.

These poems did not heal me. They did not offer *easy* answers or sudden clarity. What they did was sit with the uncertain, aching spaces inside. Slowly, writing became less about escaping the past and more about returning; not to the person I was, but to the part of me that might still be saved, still growing, still alive.

This book is born from those moments of raw and stubborn hope.
It may stumble, it may soar;
but it will never leave you alone.

Acknowledgements

This book carries pieces of all the people who made me who I am. My parents, *Shikha Gaur* and *Sanjay Gaur*, their love, unwavering support, and endless patience with my poetic ramblings have shaped everything I know about love, endurance, and even dramatic sighs.

To my sister, *Aishwarya*, who has held space for every version of me, even the ones I wish I could forget. You remind me that love can be fierce, *messy*, and deeply gentle all at once.

To *Manika*, my friend, thank you for being there for me in ways I didn't even know I needed. For listening without judgment, and for reminding me that sometimes, simply *being* is enough.

And to you, dear reader, near or far; *thank you.* This book lives because you chose to stay. I hope you find a part of yourself here.

Here's to the stories we share, come what may.

⊠. CONTENTS

SECTION A: DELUSION

We all have moments when things feel uncertain, when the lines between what we want and what's real start to blur. It's in those moments that the heart wanders, trying to make sense of the quiet noise inside. These poems are born from those in-between places.

SECTION B: LONGING & WAITING

Some waits reside longer than we expect. They stretch across seasons, memories quietly gathering as hope and heartache fold into one. These poems hold those moments of patient, aching longing.

SECTION C: LOVE IN ITS MANY SHADES

Love is never just one thing; it's a flame, a shadow, a quiet presence. These poems explore all the ways love lives inside us, bright or dim, spoken or held deep.

SECTION D: IDENTITY & INNER STRUGGLE

Our reflection is often a story half told, wrapped in layers we hide from even ourselves. These poems reach past the surface to find what's etched deep inside.

SECTION E: LOSS & GRIEF

Loss leaves a mark that doesn't fade. It's both heavy and hollow, a silence that rings the loudest. These poems face that silence, bearing its truth with quiet strength.

SECTION F: HOPE

Even in the darkest hours, there is a pulse that beats on: a quiet call to rise again. These poems carry that pulse, a soft light on the path ahead.

SECTION G: MIRROR

A space to find what's left unsaid.

1. Siren Eyes

If my eyes could take pictures,
yours would be the first,
a portrait I'd show the world:
those siren eyes, through which I read our story.

They searched for solace in every gaze,
lingering not on love, but on warmth.
They cried for companionship,
not love, not hope; only touch they craved.

I felt it,
yet held my silence.
In the quiet tilt of your gaze, I saw *you*:
the child, the weary, the lover, the son.

I chose not to breathe a word,
for faith had long deserted me.
My chances in love had faded,
and wanting you was a dream I dared *not* chase.

We shared the bench,
yet the distance stretched beyond its iron frame.

I would not let my wanting spill past my warmth;
once was lesson enough.

So I parted our eyes with a mellow goodbye,
one only silence could bind.
And I walked away,
for I had already read our story.

2. Between Silences

In shared sorrow we met,
scribbling the blots and dents.

Across the swing we sat,
humming our *mellow chorus*.

A fragile thread we weave,
of hope in sorrow's eave.

A murmured hope in night's embrace,
seeking light in this fragile space.

In whispered words unsaid,
between silences, we tread.

I wonder if you follow,
fumble, like I did, when we met.

3. Falling Without Ground

You say love is real,
but sometimes, I catch it
slipping between my fingers,
like smoke that looks solid at a glance.

I fell for you in half-shadows,
where light bends just so,
and the world didn't quite decide
if it was dream or waking.

Did you really touch me,
or was it the ghost of your breath
spiraling through my cracked window?

I'm still trying to figure out
if the warmth in my chest is yours,
or the remains of a wish,
waiting to be caught and believed.

Love feels like falling,
not into arms, but into mirrors,
where the reflection keeps shifting,
and I don't know which side is safe.

Shall I call it *madness*?
Should I be afraid,
or is it just the way
love paints its delusions
in colors too strange
to be true?

4. Three Minutes

11:47

Almost noon,
shoes on, bags waiting by the door.

The city hums its tired tune,
a soft goodbye: once, maybe more.

A scarf half-folded on the chair,
a teacup cold, a fleeting stare.

Words hover, unsure if they should fall;
we've said enough, perhaps said all.

The clock ticks louder than before,
as if it knows what's left in store.

My shadow lingers by the gate,
half willing to stay, half bound by fate.

A smile escapes, small and thin,
a trace of what *could've been.*

The lift dings once, I turn away,
the morning folds into its gray.

The sky holds nothing I can claim,
just echoes whispering *your name.*

11:50
And somehow, everything had changed.

5. Snow Angel

Let's make a snow angel;
flap your wings, or rather, your arms.
Feel yourself sink gently,
while I watch an angel take form.

With every falling flake,
I remake you in this very snow,
a quiet reminder of you:
your tilted smile,
the scar upon your right brow,
that brings back memories of our time at the beach.

Some scars remained, while others faded.
Time never healed;
I just learned to fall softer into shades
that looked just like *you*.

6. Ink & Bone

I love collecting pens
from corners of busy streets,
from quiet stores where dust sleeps,
from the hands of strangers,
and those who once called me theirs.

Each pen holds a whisper,
a story inked in silence,
crossing years and moments
like secret letters
that never reached their destination.

Some bleed blue like the ocean's *quiet sigh*,
others black as forgotten nights,
and a few, with colors bold and shy,
carry laughter, tears,
and echoes of unspoken goodbyes.

I cradle them like treasures,
not for writing,
but to remember where they came from,
the places, the faces,
the love pressed into their bones.

Each pen, a piece of the world,
waiting to script
the next story,
or simply lie still,
in the pocket of my memory.

7. Sol (Sun)

The moon was her saviour,
for the sun had betrayed.

In its light,
her heart was dismayed.

Yearning for an angel,
she embraced the *lune*.

Lord's pariah, life's unworthy;
she mourned to Sol: a soul set free.

Sol withered,
shivered,
while gloom hovered,

Rose the eclipse,
when Sol became the *Selene*.

8. Puddles at Seventeen Hundred Hours

At seventeen hundred hours,
by the crusty ochre window,
under the monochrome lamp
that cast the rain's soft dance,
sipping tea, staring at the oak tree,
"I like puddles when it rains," you whispered faintly.

I locked that moment in memory,
rains, puddles, musty oak trees;
who knew these would become my new ease.

I'd wait months for it to rain,
for tiny puddles to leap into,
springs to write you letters
beneath the very tree
you walked away from.

My love, it rained today,
the sky lit with a rainbow, vivid, bright;
what a beauty to sight.

My love, the flowers blossomed today,
purple, teal, navy, and green.
They asked if you'd return
to the seat we once shared,
the sonnet you read.
They wondered if you were truly there.

Tomorrow, not today,
you shall return,
for I cannot wait another moment,
nor bear to get drenched any longer.

In the rain, I whispered,
"My love, I liked puddles when it rained today."

9. The Cafeteria Love

Over coffee, condiments, and a cookie ajar,
Coffee and honey!
Do you want me to hate you?

Or shall we sweeten the silence,
with laughter that dances, sugar on lips,
beneath the flickering fluorescent stars?

Let's sip on dreams,
swirling stories in porcelain cups.

This bitter brew blends with sweet lies,
those moments bound with sharp goodbyes.

In the clatter and quiet, I'm torn anew.
Do I wish to burn, or to stay with you?

10. Crimson Reverie

I waited, days not hours,
autumns through fragile springs,
winters through burning summers.
On that tainted red seat,
I lay through the seasons.

By chance, circumstance, or silent coincidence,
the clock turned into daydreams.
Hoping to share the crimson,
I waited on *our* seat.

Each day drifted slowly by.
Some halted with soft concern,
some lingered, some departed,
yet none could fill the void.

With every sigh, murmur, or cry,
longing to share my warmth,
I waited on *our* seat.

11. The Waiting Hour

At six each morning,
birds lace the air with song,
a neighbor hums softly,
bicycles whisper past,
and my heart, quietly hoping.

On the cold grey slab,
scarred and bare beneath me,
I sit with a cool stone,
waiting for the first flare of sun.

With the chill drifting through,
I wish to share this day;
arms entwined,
hands held tight.

And I ask softly,
where have you been
all this while?

12. A Kept Promise

I met a guy,
blue eyes, curls rounded as if they'd embrace me just.
I barely see him, my head nearing his chest,
yet I hear him, his heart racing as I draw close.

He's joyous, or maybe I trouble him,
the latter bound to be, today or soon.
The beating falls low; steps reverse through time,
long gone shall he be, for trouble is what I carry.

Nothing reaches me but the infinite dark;
the momentous light far gone,
farther than I can feel.

I hold hands with *gloom*, loyal of all companions,
a kept promise, not him and me,
but *Gloom and I.*

I shall walk ahead,
dressed in dark, chauffeured by gloom.
We stay close,
gloom and I.

13. Shadow's Tint

In a room lined with faces,
in a space where silence traces,
with fear painted sharp,
I hear: feet steady, unfazed.
I watch across the door.

Etched in black,
the leather shining,
through the dark,
your shadow smiled.

Beneath the weight of whispered breath,
your shadow moves with *silent death*.
No words escape, no light reveals,
just echoes where the darkness steals.

Your figure framed in fractured light,
a puzzle shaped in fading night.
I stand unmoved, a silent lore,
guarding secrets behind the door.

14. Mountains We Never Saw

Mountains.
The ones we sketched together,
the last we loved.

A train to the hills,
a room to stay,
some vine to sip,
some snow to play.

Pebbles so safe,
I keep till late.
A trip to the mountains,
I'd love to take.

The whisper of pines,
the sky's endless blue,
footprints in snow,
a path made for two.

The echo of laughter,
the warmth of a fire,
moments like these
lift my heart higher.

A trip to the mountains,
where *dreams never fade*,
caught in a moment,
a memory made.

15. Love, Unseen

In every life,
you'll find me loving you,
from tiniest creature,
to mammoth or few.

Beyond the stars,
beneath the sun's light,
I hold you close
in day and in night.

I walk beside you,
both near and far,
a steady flame,
your constant star.

In rustling leaves,
and ocean's song,
in right and wrong,
where hearts belong.

No shape, no time,
can break this thread,
the soul recalls
the words once said.

And when the world
grows dark and cold,
my love remains,
a hand to hold.

For life may fade,
and time may end,
but love, my dear,
will always *ascend*.

16. Lemonade's 1.10

"Lemonade's 1.10
Would you like some?"

Glittery billboard,
chalk smudged,
sunlight on your skin,
brighter than the morning within.

I watched you laugh,
a tilt of your head,
hair catching the breeze,
and something inside me
started to *fizz*,
like soda shaken too hard,
bubbling over, sweet and sharp.

"Make it two," I whispered,
voice unsure,
balancing on the edge
of daring and delight.

Tart lemon with sugar,
glances shrinking the street
to a corner of warmth
and quiet heat.

Fingers curl around the cup,
palms brushing,
like liquid gold,
too bright to grasp,
too fleeting to release.

And when you smiled again,
I knew some flavors
were meant to sting a little,
to linger,
and make the heart remember
even after the last drop was gone.

17. Canvas

Your painted face, so *bold*, so *true*,
speaks not in words, but every *hue*,
a canvas laid, presenting your *soul*.

In shadows deep, where colors blend,
trade my *light* for visions penned.
Each stroke reveals the *whispers shared*,
a bond of silence, *souls ensnared*.

What secrets lie in every *shade*?
In you, my heart's *reflection played*.
Upon this canvas, *stark* and *bold*,
the story of two *spirits* told.

I wonder, what *cost*?
Selling my *soul* to only see yours.

Sombre as is,
your *soul* I say,
to see your *soul*,
I sell my *veil*.

18. Prisms of You

Love is a *prism*,
bent across the edge of us,
fracturing sunlight into colors
we did not know we carried.

The *gold* of morning warmth,
when your hand finds mine
and the world hums quietly
between our heartbeats.

The deep *violet* of longing,
when miles stretch for years,
and every message unread
feels like a winter evening indoors, alone.

There is the *red* of anger,
hot and sharp,
clashing with words unsaid,
and the bitter taste of pride.

There is the *blue* of nostalgia,
soft and dripping,
the echo of old songs
and the smell of your coat in the closet.

Yet every shade,
every break and bend of light,
is proof that we exist in *spectrum*,
that love is never one color,
but *all colors*,
and sometimes, the spaces in between.

19. Veil of Blue

I'm writing my tale from beneath the ocean,
where the sun fades and rises anew.

I'm drowning, *yet not suffering;*
perhaps this is peace in its bluest shade.

Ocean wide with silver waves,
moonlit shade upon the waves.

I'm writing my tale from beneath the ocean,
where I'm next to myself; bare skin, pale and serene.

My hair mimicking the wave, my hands, no longer
writing the tale.
I look up to the *lune*, smiling silver, confiding in its elegy.

I say I'm drowning, *yet not suffering;*
I'm writing my tale from beneath the ocean.

20. Kafkaesque

Kafka and I shared a tale,
of reality and illusion,
both muddled, both gory.

"Franz, is he alive?" I ask.
"Mere physical," he offers.

"Franz, will he ever rise?
Quietly, every day, unseen."

Drowning, is he, I wonder,
not the protagonist, or the creation;
will the creator live?

I flip the page.
Kafka and I shared a tale;
"Not my way," said his rage.

21. By the Tree House

Find me next to the *dusty tree house*
where I last sat, praising the Lord
and the life *she gave.*

Feet on the icy loam
one hand draped on the bright carved bar
eyes staring beyond,
holding onto a faith *worn yet fierce.*

Praise the Lord, I said
my closest companion, my strongest armour
but today felt different
a whisper of doubt crept under the skin.

With feet still grounded
my mind began to wander
questioning not just *her choices*
but the loneliness that wrapped around me like a
shadow.

I wanted to resist the creeping dark
to hold firm the armour of belief
but my thoughts teemed with doubt
hatred and that infamous *gloom.*

Not the serene night I've sat under for years
this dusk was heavier, gloomier
thick with a silent plea to *give up.*

My heart wavered, almost ready to throw it all away
standing against the tides
no longer *us* against the world
but *me against her alone.*

I always sat here alone
but today I was *truly alone.*

Am I so far gone? I wondered
while I stepped down
our dusty tree house.

22. Pariah's Coly

Sun set, rose midnight
turned rays into dim light.

Thick ice, breath suspended
I sat in solitude
mocking the ever-moving.

"Pariah to the land," said they
"Lone wolf," said I.

Sitting in solitude, mocking the ever-moving
laughed I
not in sorrow, or in joy
but in knowing
I belonged to *neither*.

23. Home

They say forests bear life.
passing through the squally winds,
I wonder if it is true,
I wonder if *silence talks.*

Watching closely, I figured;
the language of the greens:
yellow, ochre passing through the blue,
I spoke to the greens.

Through the darkness ran the light of hope,
hope to witness its full extent.
I chased, fell, tumbled, and humbled all too soon,
tracing aurora's trail, I reached

a place where I stood numb
poised towards the blue, eyes shut with the longest sigh.
I was there, I was home,
within the extent of the greens, I was *lone.*

24. Death

If death shall come,
make it come easy, *Lord,*
for dying every day is harder still.

Alone, I wandered through nights,
chasing ghosts of who I was,
lost between hope and despair.

I have carried burdens unseen,
heavy as grief upon my chest,
longing for gentle release,
yearning for peace to rest.

I beg for quiet ease,
a final breath, a quiet close.

If death shall come,
make it come easy, *Lord.*

25. Glitter Jitter Conundrum

Glitter-colored light
or a mere jitter?
Every three they shut
it latches on to me.

Dark, bloody yet bright
the light catches onto me
every time my eyes shut,
the *veils latch on to me*.

Echoes of laughter
flickers of distant glee
every shadow that lingers
whispers softly, *"Set me free."*

Glimmers fade and shimmer
a dance of what could be
each moment spins around me
and time, it holds the key.

Caught between flickers
trapped inside this gleam
the light and dark tether
pulling at my dream.

Million, billion, and zillion
memories latch on to me
every three I shut my eyes
my dark catches on to me.

26. A Night Painted in Hues

Tonight is a night painted in hues.
Lying on this bare ground,
resting my head against the grass,
I trace Orion, the one true link
between stories shared and those left unspoken.

The stars share secrets in *silver*,
strands of old dreams woven tight.
While the cool breeze hums its gentle tune,
a lullaby beneath a silent moon.

Tonight will happen never,
for tonight is the only night.
A silence deep that no one breaks,
a weight of time that slowly aches.

Here, in this still hour,
love blooms quiet like a hidden flower.
Soft and steady, deeply true,
in every shade of every *hue*.

27. Pigeon

With wings that could fly,
to live like a pigeon caged,
such is to be a lover *unloved*.

Watching the rain drizzle, the wind wander,
the sky dull, the stars shine,
was I meant to fly, or merely bleed?

With wings that could fly,
I live like a pigeon caged,
heart beating against iron bars,
such is to be a lover *unloved*.

I trace the flight of birds in endless skies,
their freedom a blade that cuts and sighs.
Trapped beneath glass, yearning to soar,
to be unloved is to ache at the core.

To live like a pigeon, bound and confined,
with dreams of a sky I'll never find.
Oh, what cruel fate to long and grieve,
to love unseen, to never receive.

28. Herz (Heart)

Serene as that winter night,
sombre like a midnight song,
still is the heart that once sang
a *coly* romance.

Quiet as a writer's mind,
questioning like a lover's pride,
pale is the heart
that once blazed *scarlet*.

Silent as the falling snow,
tender as a whispered vow,
cold is the soul
that once burned bright.

Lonely as a forgotten song,
dark as a shadow stretching long,
empty is the heart
that once danced along.

29. Oh, to Be Loved

Oh, to be loved,
not as a pawn in some cruel game,
not just a flicker before the abyss swallows *flame*,
but as flesh that trembles,
as bone that does not crumble
beneath the weight of fear or *shame*.

Yet this skin of doubt and despair
clings like a cage woven from longing and *care*.
Each heartbeat becomes a dirge
for a love that never wakes,
a silent *surge*
in a forsaken chamber's air.

And still I reach
for the empty space beside me,
fingers brushing, *pleading*,
finding only the echo of what could have been,
and never leaving.

30. Watching with Death

The ink has risen, as I mourn your death.
I meet death's eyes, steady, unflinching, true.

Darkest tint of black, loudest wails of cry,
and still, I envy death.

I envy death, for it watches me despair, for you.
It holds you close,
while I clutch only what's left of you.

Tonight I wonder
If befriending death, will lead me near,
let me hear your voice once more,
love you, just once more.

I feel dejected, or do I?
You've trailed toward the blue,
a brighter place, you see.

You live in light,
while I lament with the *loon.*

31. The Quiet Night (Knight)

In darkened halls of stone and night,
a weary knight upholds the fight.
No sword, no shout commands the way,
but quiet will that will not sway.

Dragons slumber in stories told,
yet fire burns in hearts so *bold*.
No shining crown, no lofty throne,
just strength in silence made her own.

While queens and sages wage their wars,
the humble write their quiet scars.
Not glory's cry, but steady hand
makes strong the soul, hearts that withstand.

In darkened halls of stone and night,
a weary knight endures the fight.

32. By the Willows

Under the willow tree
by your woodland house,
you promised me a life,
a vision I could barely bind.

A large swing in the garden,
the worn 90s waddle chair,
a shelf you'd build for my
outrageous mugs, without a care.

By the lake, you promised
a well full of will,
fishes swimming in sync,
and dishes blushing in pink.

"Fool, to wish and want,"
my mother sighs and warns.

If only she knew you like I do,
had faith as I had.
If only she believed you'd come home true.

It's lunch o'clock,
I'll write to you again at dinner, at dawn.
My love, my reminder:
you promised me home,
a shelf and well,
some fishes in sync.
I'd hate to wash the dishes plain.

33. A Beautiful Crime

I was never a tea person,
until you passed me that chipped cup,
steam curling between us at that serene dawn.

I feared bikes,
until you matched my pace for miles;
no rush, no words, just wheels and unwind.

I thought I hated being loved,
till you brought me the lilacs: purple and unasked,
a quiet rebellion against my silence.

Is this infatuation, affection, or love?
Who am I to name it? What even is a lover?
To give your heart is brave,
but to receive one, that's a risk worth trembling over.

And if it wasn't meant for me all along?
If pieces were already gone?
Then let this be ritual anyway.
Because loving may be easy,
but to be loved?
That's a *beautiful crime.*

34. Full of You

I hate blank pages.
They mirror the silence between *"I'm fine"* and truth,
the way we learned to speak in half-lights,
close enough to touch, yet drowning in soft plights.

A field of unsaid apologies, small aches,
spaces where sentences fold back, unfinished.
Unwritten confessions spill quietly;
in between my hands, the paper waits.

Each quiet moment gathers itself,
until emptiness becomes its own kind of presence.
And every bit of space here,
it's full of what's missing,
but somehow, it is how I know *you're near.*

And yet,
if love is measured in absences,
then yes,
this room is full of *you.*

35. From Red to Ink

I bleed ink now,
after bleeding red.
Veins run empty,
life quietly *bled*.

Shadows soften
with every line drawn,
from pain's cold ashes
new dreams are born.

This ink will weave
what blood once erased,
a silent strength,
in shadows *encased*.

Each word spills truth
from the hollow within,
etching scars into art,
turning sorrow to skin.

Pages borrrow my grief,
holding whispers and sighs,
turning my lost,
into wings that rise.

36. Hope in the Night

When the night is dark and cold,
Hope is a light that's quietly *bold*.
It's not a shout or a flame,
but a soft glow, your gentle *name*.

Etched deep,
a forever mark that makes me whole.
It stays through storms and quiet hours,
a hidden strength, a quiet power.

Quick and bright, like *ink in light*,
fading soon, but shining in the night.
A fleeting spark, a truth we hold,
a story whispered, brave and *bold*.

The night is long and stretches far,
yet hope remains my guiding star.
It creeps through shadows, calm and deep,
a promise kept while others sleep.

In darkened hours, hope will find
the cracks where light can slip and bind.
It grows in silence, slow but sure,
a patient heart that will endure.

Though night envelopes round and tight,
hope is always near our sight.
In every tremble, tear, and every fight,
hope is the mark **etched or inked** every night.

37. Prelude to You

Every soul hides a dark veil;
Quiet, unseen.

The next page is for *You*,
For your soul to speak.

Let the inner writer flow through,
Scribble, write and lament,
what you never could before.

38. Poem:

....
To you,
My masked poet,
I hear you; loud and clear.

39.

Until Next Time..
Promise I won't do this again, wink wink ✦